POETRY

— TO —

MAKE
YOU
SMILE

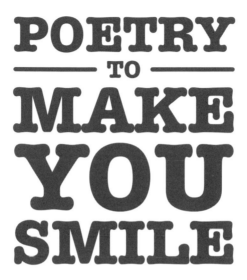

POETRY TO MAKE YOU SMILE

Introduced by Jane O. Wayne

spruce

Contents

Preface

7

Preface

The 100 poems selected here to make us smile show that indeed one finds lightness in unexpected places. From sexual to religious ecstasy, anything can make us smile, and does in this collection. For example, the wit of Robert Frost's short lines and odd rhymes and rhythms turn a minor mishap ("I stepped on the toe/ of an unemployed hoe") into an amusement.

The poems in the book move through a wide range of experience—the ups and downs of family life; the vagaries of love and marriage; the quirks of creatures real and imagined; our comic exasperation over things gone awry; the eccentricities of various whimsical characters; our grand passions for food and drink; the absurdities of youth and age; and finally—the spontaneous delight of just being in the world.

WC Fields once said, "Start every day with a smile and get it over with," and we laugh at the maxim turned on end, laugh at what we hope is a cynical persona. For who doesn't enjoy the relief of a giggle, a laugh, a moment's smile?

A poet's hand can turn a subject on its head, or simply turn it a few degrees, and make us smile. Smiles and laughter are powerful forces in life, as Mark Twain knew when he said "Against the assault of laughter nothing can stand."

I won't spoil your pleasure (like some movie preview showing the best, and sometimes only, jokes) by giving away the punch-lines, those surprises, and discoveries that you'll make yourself. Read on.

Jane O. Wayne

Daddy fell into the pond

Everyone grumbled. The sky was grey.
We had nothing to do and nothing to say.
We were nearing the end of a dismal day,
And then there seemed to be nothing beyond,
Then
Daddy fell into the pond!

And everyone's face grew merry and bright,
And Timothy danced for sheer delight.
"Give me the camera, quick, oh quick!
He's crawling out of the duckweed!" Click!

Then the gardener suddenly slapped his knee,
And doubled up, shaking silently,
And the ducks all quacked as if they were daft,
And it sounded as if the old drake laughed.
Oh, there wasn't a thing that didn't respond
When
Daddy fell into the pond!

Alfred Noyes

The fathers

Traditionally, the same actor plays Captain Hook
and Mr. Darling.
      — The Picture Book of Peter Pan (c. 1930)

Something's familiar about that villain
striding the deck of the Jolly Roger, chest
puffed out under the fancy jabot —
a bit like, yes, like Father huffing around
before an evening out, proper shirtfront
outthrust by an important bay window.
Particular about his cuff links as a pirate
about lace at his wrists. Same air of dashing
yet dastardly middle age. A penchant
for issuing orders and threats, and tying
up uncooperative dogs or Indian princesses.

No wonder we sons and daughters laugh
when Hook sits on the hot toadstool
over Peter's chimney, when Tinker Bell
flits out of his grasp. And especially
at his slapstick flailing through the sea,
pursued by that confident long-jawed beast,
time ticking loud in its belly.

Elizabeth Holmes

After making love we hear footsteps

For I can snore like a bullhorn
or play loud music
or sit up talking with any reasonably sober Irishman
and Fergus will only sink deeper
into his dreamless sleep, which goes by all in one flash,
but let there be that heavy breathing
or a stifled come-cry anywhere in the house
and he will wrench himself awake
and make for it on the run – as now, we lie together,
after making love, quiet, touching along the length of our
    bodies,
familiar touch of the long-married,
and he appears – in his baseball pajamas, it happens,
the neck opening so small
he has to screw them on, which one day may make him
    wonder
about the mental capacity of baseball players –
and flops down between us and hugs us and snuggles
    himself to sleep,
his face gleaming with satisfaction at being this very child.
In the half darkness we look at each other
and smile
and touch arms across his little, startling muscled body –
this one whom habit of memory propels to the ground of
his making,
sleeper only the mortal sounds can sing awake,
this blessing love gives again into our arms.

Galway Kinnell

12

Fault

In the airport bar, I tell my mother not to worry.
No one ever tripped and fell into the San Andreas
Fault. But as she dabs at her dry eyes, I remember
those old movies where the earth does open.

There's always one blonde entomologist, four
deceitful explorers, and a pilot who's good-looking
but not smart enough to take off his leather jacket
in the jungle.

Still, he and Dr. Cutie Bug are the only ones
who survive the spectacular quake because
they spent their time making plans to go back
to the Mid-West and live near his parents

while the others wanted to steal the gold and ivory
then move to Los Angeles where they would rarely
call their mothers and almost never fly home
and when they did for only a few days at a time.

Ron Koertge

Mother doesn't want a dog

Mother doesn't want a dog.
Mother says they smell,
And never sit when you say sit,
Or even when you yell.
And when you come home late at night
And there is ice and snow,
You have to go back out because
The dumb dog has to go.

Mother doesn't want a dog.
Mother says they shed,
And always let the strangers in
And bark at friends instead,
And do disgraceful things on rugs,
And track mud on the floor,
And flop upon your bed at night
And snore their doggy snore.

Mother doesn't want a dog.
She's making a mistake.
Because, more than a dog, I think
She will not want this snake.

Judith Viorst

Snow

Walking through a field with my little brother Seth

I pointed to a place where kids had made angels in the
    snow.
For some reason, I told him that a troop of angels
had been shot and dissolved when they hit the ground.

He asked who had shot them and I said a farmer.
Then we were on the roof of the lake.
The ice looked like a photograph of water.

Why he asked. Why did he shoot them.

I didn't know where I was going with this.

They were on his property, I said.
When it's snowing, the outdoors seem like a room.

Today I traded hellos with my neighbor.
Our voices hung close in the new acoustics.
A room with the walls blasted to shreds and falling.

We returned to our shoveling, working side by side in
    silence.

But why were they on his property, he asked.

David Berman

Her latest flame

My sister drags her boyfriends home to meet us
Subjects them all to family scrutiny
They disappear for hours up in her bedroom
Then disappear for ever after tea

Where love's concerned, Ella is like a Mountie
Fierce and direct, she always gets her boy
Dad says that she's a 'shameless little hussy',
Dumping each suitor like a broken toy

Ella can't see what we all find so funny
Boys are like fish to her, there's plenty more
Love is a game to girls like Ella
Perhaps it's because she's only four

Lindsay Macrae

The chatterbox

From morning till night it was Lucy's delight
To chatter and talk without stopping:
There was not a day but she rattled away,
Like water for ever a-dropping.
No matter at all if the subjects were small,
Or not worth the trouble of saying,
'Twas equal to her, she would talking prefer
To working, or reading, or playing.
You'll think now, perhaps, that there would have been
     gaps,
If she had not been wonderfully clever:
That her sense was so great, and so witty her pate,
It would be forthcoming forever;
But that's quite absurd, for have you not heard
That much tongue and few brains are connected?
That they are supposed to think least who talk most,
And their wisdom is always suspected?
While Lucy was young, had she bridled her tongue,
With a little good sense and exertion,
Who knows, but she might now have been our delight,
Instead of our jest and aversion?

Ann Taylor

In praise of zigzags

For a Girl Failing Geometry

Maybe she does her homework
the way she does her chores.
She moves quickly when she vacuums,
forgetting corners in the living room,
repeating others,
zigzags recklessly across the carpet,
raising those pale tracks
behind her in the wool, crossing
and recrossing them. And not once
does geometry cross her mind.
Outside she wanders aimlessly
behind the lawnmower,
rolls toward the middle of the lawn,
then doubles back.
For a while, she'll follow straight lines –
the fence, the hedge, the walk –
then go off on a tangent, spiraling
around the birch or the maple.
When she finishes,
she leaves the lawnmower out, leaves
a trail of unmown strips and crisscrosses,
her scribbling on the lawn
like a line of thought that's hard to follow.
As far as she's concerned
the shortest distance between two points
is confining.

Jane O. Wayne

18

praise song

to my aunt blanche
who rolled from grass to driveway
into the street one sunday morning.
i was ten. i had never seen
a human woman hurl her basketball
of a body into the traffic of the world.
Praise to the drivers who stopped in time.
Praise to the faith with which she rose
after some moments then slowly walked
sighing back to her family.
Praise to the arms which understood
little or nothing of what it meant
but welcomed her in without judgment,
accepting it all like children might,
like God.

Lucille Clifton

Dishwater

Slap of the screen door, flat knock
of my grandmother's boxy black shoes
on the wooden stoop, the hush and sweep
of her knob-kneed, cotton-aproned stride
out to the edge and then, toed in
with a furious twist and heave,
a bridge that leaps from her hot red hands
and hangs there shining for fifty years
over the mystified chickens,
over the swaying nettles, the ragweed,
the clay slope down to the creek,
over the redwing blackbirds in the tops.

Ted Kooser

Love's philosophy

The fountains mingle with the river
  And the rivers with the Ocean,
The winds of Heaven mix for ever
  With a sweet emotion;
Nothing in the world is single;
  All things by a law divine
In one spirit meet and mingle,
  Why not I with thine? –

See the mountains kiss high Heaven
  And the waves clasp one another;
No sister-flower would be forgiven
  If it disdained its brother;
And the sunlight clasps the earth
  And the moonbeams kiss the sea:
What is all this sweet work worth
  If thou kiss not me?

Percy Bysshe Shelley

Office friendships

Eve is madly in love with Hugh
And Hugh is keen on Jim.
Charles is in love with very few
And few are in love with him.

Myra sits typing notes of love
With romantic pianist's fingers.
Dick turns his eyes to the heavens above
Where Fran's divine perfume lingers.

Nicky is rolling eyes and tits
And flaunting her wiggly walk
Everybody is thrilled to bits
By Clive's suggestive talk.

Sex suppressed will go berserk,
But it keeps us all alive.
It's a wonderful change from wives and work.
And it ends at half past five.

Gavin Ewart

I'm really very fond

I'm really very fond of you,
he said.
I don't like fond.
It sounds like something
you would tell a dog.
Give me love,
or nothing.
Throw your fond in a pond,
I said.
But what I felt for him
was also warm, frisky,
moist-mouthed,
eager, and could swim away
if forced to do so.

Alice Walker

How to change a frog into a prince

Start with the underwear. Sit him down.
Hopping on one leg may stir unpleasant memories.
If he gets his tights on, even backwards, praise him.
Fingers, formerly webbed, struggle over buttons.
Arms and legs, lengthened out of proportion, wait,
as you do, for the rest of him to catch up.
This body, so recently reformed, reclaimed,
still carries the marks of its time as a frog. Be gentle.
Avoid the words awkward and gawky.
Do not use tadpole as a term of endearment.
His body, like his clothing, may seem one size too big.
Relax. There's time enough for crowns. He'll grow into it.

Anna Denise

Green frog at Roadstead, Wisconsin

It is the way of a pleasant path
To walk through white birch, fir,
And spruce on a limestone trail
Through the quiet, complacent time
Of summer when, suddenly, the frog jumps
And you jump after him, laughing,
Hopping, frog and woman, to show
The stationary world its flat ways.
Love is a Frog, I grin that greenly
To your green eyes and they leap
At me. Up, I will enter the Frog World
With you and try the leaping ways
Of the heart that we do not fail to find
The sunlit air full of leaping chances.

James Schevill

True love

It is true love because
I put on eyeliner and a concerto and make pungent
observations about the great
issues of the day
Even when there's no one here but him,
And because
I do not resent watching the Green Bay Packer
Even though I am philosophically opposed to football,
And because
When he is late for dinner and I know he must be either
having an affair or
lying dead in the middle of the street,
I always hope he's dead.
It's true love because
If he said quit drinking martinis but I kept drinking them
and the next morning I
couldn't get out of bed,
He wouldn't tell me he told me,
And because
He is willing to wear unironed undershorts
Out of respect for the fact that I am philosophically
opposed to ironing,
And because
If his mother was drowning and I was drowning and he
had to choose one of
us to save,
He says he'd save me.

When he went to San Francisco on business while I
had to stay home with the painters and the
exterminator and the baby who was getting the chicken
        pox,
He understood why I hated him,
And because
When I said that playing the stock market was
juvenile and irresponsible and then the stock I
wouldn't let him buy went up twenty-six points,
I understood why he hated me,
And because
Despite cigarette cough, tooth decay, acid
indigestion, dandruff, and other features of
married life that tend to dampen the fires of passion,
We still feel something
We can call
True love.

Judith Viorst

Fight

That is the difference between me and you.
You pack an umbrella, #30 sun goo
And a red flannel shirt. That's not what I do.

I put the top down as soon as we arrive.
The temperature's trying to pass fifty-five.
I'm freezing but at least I'm alive.

Nothing on earth can diminish my glee.
This is Florida, Florida, land of euphoria,
Florida in the highest degree.

You dig in the garden. I swim in the pool.
I like to wear cotton. You like to wear wool.
You're always hot. I'm usually cool.

You want to get married. I want to be free.
You don't seem to mind that we disagree.
And that is the difference between you and me.

Laurel Blossom.

Flowers in the kitchen

On buying her flowers
she said

"There's no food in the kitchen
and we can't eat flowers."

On buying her food
she said

"You don't buy flowers any more."

Lemn Sissay

A piazza tragedy

The beauteous Ethel's father has a
Newly painted front piazza,
    He has a
    Piazza;
When with tobacco juice 'twas tainted,
They had the front piazza painted,
    That tainted
    Piazza painted.

Algernon called that night, perchance,
Arrayed in comely sealskin pants,
    That night, perchance,
    In gorgeous pants;
Engaging Ethel in a chat
On that piazza down he sat,
    In chat

    They sat.

And when an hour or two had passed,
He tried to rise, but oh, stuck fast
    At last
    Stuck fast!
Fair Ethel shrieked, "It is the paint!"
And fainted in a deadly faint,
    This saint
    Did faint.

Algernon sits there to this day,
He cannot tear himself away;
    Away?
    Nay, nay,
His pants are firm, the paint is dry,
He's nothing else to do but die;
    To die!
    O my!

Eugene Field

Fair's fair now, Venus...

Fair's fair now, Venus. This girl's got me hooked.
All I'm asking from her
Is love – or at least some future hope for my own
Eternal devotion. No, even that's too much – hell, just let
    me love her!
(Listen, Venus: I've asked you so often now.)
Say yes, pet. I'd be your slave for years, for a lifetime.
Say yes   unswerving fidelity's my strong suit.
I may not have top-drawer connections, I can't produce
    blue-blooded
Ancestors to impress you, my father's plain middle-class,
And there aren't any squads of ploughmen to deal with
    my broad acres –
My parents are both pretty thrifty, and need to be.
What have I got on my side, then? Poetic genius,
    sweetheart,
Divine inspiration. And love. I'm yours to command –
Unswerving faithfulness, morals above suspicion
Naked simplicity, a born-to-the-purple blush.
I don't chase thousands of girls, I'm no sexual circus-rider;
Honestly, all I want is to look after you
Till death do us part, have the two of us living together
All my time, and know you'll cry for me when I'm gone.
Besides, when you give me yourself, what you'll be
    providing
Is creative material. My art will rise to the theme

And immortalize you. Look, why do you think we
    remember
The swan-upping of Leda, or Io's life as a cow,
Or poor virgin Europa whisked off overseas, clutching
That so-called bull by the-horn? Through poems, of
    course.
So you and I, love, will enjoy that same world-wide
    publicity,
And our names will be linked, forever, with the gods.

Ovid
(Translated from the Latin by Peter Green)

"I love you sweatheart"

A man risked his life to write the words.
A man hung upside down (an idiot friend
holding his legs?) with spray paint
to write the words on a girder fifty feet above
a highway. And his beloved,
the next morning driving to work…?
His words are not (meant to be) so unique.
Does she recognize his handwriting?
Did he hint to her at her doorstep the night before
of "something special, darling, tomorrow"?
And did he call her at work
expecting her to faint with delight
at his celebration of her, his passion, his risk?
She will know I love her now,
the world will know my love for her!
A man risked his life to write the world.
Love is like this at the bone, we hope, love
is like this, Sweatheart, all sore and dumb
and dangerous, ignited, blessed—always,
regardless, no exceptions,
always in blazing matters like these: blessed.

Thomas Lux

Valentine

Chipmunks jump, and
Greensnakes slither.
Rather burst than
Not be with her.

Bluebirds fight, but
Bears are stronger.
We've got fifty
Years or longer.

Hoptoads hop, but
Hogs are fatter.
Nothing else but
Us can matter.

Donald Hall

Two lovers make love despite their sunburns

With motion slow and gingerly they place
Their outward forms, broiled bright as carapace,
Like linesmen handling bared high-tension wires,
Dreading the surges of abrupt desires.

X. J. Kennedy

"What do women want?"

I want a red dress.
I want it flimsy and cheap,
I want it too tight, I want to wear it
until someone tears it off me.
I want it sleeveless and backless,
this dress, so no one has to guess
what's underneath. I want to walk down
the street past Thrifty's and the hardware store
with all those keys glittering in the window,
past Mr. and Mrs. Wong selling day-old
donuts in their café, past the Guerra brothers
slinging pigs from the truck and onto the dolly,
hoisting the slick snouts over their shoulders.
I want to walk like I'm the only
woman on earth and I can have my pick.
I want that red dress bad.
I want it to confirm
your worst fears about me,
to show you how little I care about you
or anything except what
I want. When I find it, I'll pull that garment
from its hanger like I'm choosing a body
to carry me into this world, through
the birth-cries and the love-cries too,
and I'll wear it like bones, like skin,
it'll be the goddamned
dress they bury me in.

Kim Addonizio

Personal

I want a man whose body makes mine hum,
who when he looks my way the sky goes hazy.
Don't call me if you're boring, crude or dumb.

Discussions about sports teams turn me numb,
and men who can't stop talking drive me crazy.
I want a man whose body makes mine hum,

who sweetly cries my name out as we come,
a sensual man, whose touch makes me feel dizzy.
Don't call me if you're angry, cheap or dumb.

I like full lips, bare skin, long winter nights, some
good red wine. I like to spend a lazy
morning with a man who makes me hum.

I like to wade in fountains just for fun,
to decorate my hairband with a daisy,
skinny-dipping, hopscotch, playing dumb.

I love good jazz, dancing till I'm numb,
deep snow, strong wind, a girl dressed up in paisley.
I want a man whose body makes mine hum.
Don't call me if you're rigid, mean or dumb.

Beth Gylys

Be quiet, Sir!

Be quiet, Sir! Begone, I say!
Lord bless us! How you romp and tear!
There!
I swear!
Now you left my bosom bare!
I do not like such boisterous play,
So take that saucy hand away –
Why now, you're ruder than before!
Nay, I'll be hanged if I comply –
Fie!
I'll cry!
Oh – I can't bear it – I shall die!
I vow I'll never see you more!
But – are you sure you've shut the door?

Anonymous

One perfect rose

A single flow'r he sent me, since we met.
All tenderly his messenger he chose;
Deep-hearted, pure, with scented dew still wet –
One perfect rose.

I knew the language of the floweret;
"My fragile leaves," it said, "his heart enclose."
Love long has taken for his amulet
One perfect rose.

Why is it no one ever sent me yet
One perfect limousine, do you suppose?
Ah no, it's always just my luck to get
One perfect rose.

Dorothy Parker

To my laundress

Saponacea, wert thou not so fair
I'd curse thee for thy multitude of sins –
For sending home my clothes all full of pins,
A shirt occasionally that's a snare
And a delusion, got, the Lord knows where,
The Lord knows why, a sock whose outs and ins
None knows, nor where it ends nor where begins,
And fewer cuffs than ought to be my share.
But when I mark thy lilies how they grow,
And the red roses of thy ripening charms,
I bless the lovelight in thy dark eyes dreaming.
I'll never pay thee, but I'd gladly go
Into the magic circle of thine arms,
Supple and fragrant from repeated steaming.

Ambrose Bierce

Sorrows of Werther

Werther had a love for Charlotte
Such as words could never utter;
Would you know how first he met her?
She was cutting bread and butter.
Charlotte was a married lady,
And a moral man was Werther,
And, for all the wealth of Indies,
Would do nothing for to hurt her.
So he sighed and pined and ogled,
And his passion boiled and bubbled,
Till he blew his silly brains out,
And no more was by it troubled.
Charlotte, having seen his body
Borne before her on a shutter,
Like a well-conducted person,
Went on cutting bread and butter.

William Makepeace Thackeray

The ichthyosaurus

There once was an Ichthyosaurus,
Who lived when the earth was all porous,
But he fainted with shame
When he first heard his name,
And departed a long time before us.

Isabel Frances Bellows

The sloth

        In moving-slow he has no Peer.
You ask him something in his Ear,
He thinks about it for a Year;
And, then, before he says a Word
There, upside down (unlike a Bird),
He will assume that you have Heard –
A most Ex-as-per-at-ing Lug.
But should you call his manner Smug,
He'll sigh and give his Branch a Hug;
Then off again to Sleep he goes,
Still swaying gently by his Toes,
And you just know he knows he knows.

Theodore Roethke

Upon a snail

She goes but softly, but she goeth sure,
She stumbles not, as stronger creatures do.
Her journey's shorter, so she may endure
Better than they which do much farther go.
She makes no noise, but stilly seizeth on
The flower or herb appointed for her food,
The which she quietly doth feed upon
While others range and glare, but find no good.
And though she doth but very softly go,
However, 'tis not fast nor slow, but sure;
And certainly they that do travel so,
The prize they do aim at they do procure.

John Bunyan

Eine kleine snailmusik

"The snail watchers are interested in snails from all angles .... At the moment they are investigating the snail's reaction to music. 'We have played to them on the harp in the garden and in the country on the pipe,' said Mr. Heaton, 'and we have taken them into the house and played to them on the piano.'"
- *The London Star.*

What soothes the angry snail?
What's music to his horn?
For the "Sonata Appassionata,"
He shows scorn,
And Handel
Makes the frail snail
Quail,
While Prokofieff
Gets no laugh
And Tschaikowsky, I fear,
No tear.

Piano, pipe, and harp,
Dulcet or shrill,
Flat or sharp,
Indoors or in the garden,
Are willy-nilly
Silly
To the reserved, slow,
Sensitive
Snail,
Who prefers to live
Glissandissimo,
Pianissimo.

May Sarton

Heaven

Fish (fly-replete, in depth of June,
Dawdling away their wat'ry noon)
Ponder deep wisdom, dark or clear,
Each secret fishy hope or fear.
Fish say, they have their Stream and Pond;
But is there anything Beyond?
This life cannot be All, they swear,
For how unpleasant, if it were!
One may not doubt that, somehow, Good
Shall come of Water and of Mud;
And, sure, the reverent eye must see
A Purpose in Liquidity.
We darkly know, by Faith we cry,
The future is not Wholly Dry.
Mud unto mud! – Death eddies near –
Not here the appointed End, not here!
But somewhere, beyond Space and Time.
Is wetter water, slimier slime!
And there (they trust) there swimmeth One
Who swam ere rivers were begun,
Immense, of fishy form and mind,
Squamous, omnipotent, and kind;
And under that Almighty Fin,
The littlest fish may enter in.
Oh! never fly conceals a hook,
Fish say, in the Eternal Brook,
But more than mundane weeds are there,

And mud, celestially fair;
Fat caterpillars drift around,
And Paradisal grubs are found;
Unfading moths, immortal flies,
And the worm that never dies.
And in that Heaven of all their wish,
There shall be no more land, say fish.

Rupert Brooke

The rabbit

The rabbit has a charming face:
Its private life is a disgrace.
I really dare not name to you
The awful things that rabbits do;
Things that your paper never prints –
You only mention them in hints.
They have such lost, degraded souls
No wonder they inhabit holes;
When such depravity is found
It only can live underground.

Anonymous

Alley cat love song

Come into the garden, Fred,
For the neighborhood tabby is gone.
Come into the garden, Fred.
I have nothing but my flea collar on,
And the scent of catnip has gone to my head.
I'll wait by the screen door till dawn.

The fireflies court in the sweetgum tree.
The nightjar calls from the pine,
And she seems to say in her rhapsody,
"Oh, mustard-brown Fred, be mine!"
The full moon lights my whiskers afire,
And the fur goes erect on my spine.

I hear the frogs in the muddy lake
Croaking from shore to shore.
They've one swift season to soothe their ache.
In autumn they sing no more.
So ignore me now, and you'll hear my meow
As I scratch all night at the door

Dana Gioia

She sights a Bird – she chuckles –

She sights a Bird – she chuckles –
She flattens – then she crawls –
She runs without the look of feet –
Her eyes increase to Balls –
Her Jaws stir – twitching – hungry –
Her Teeth can hardly stand –
She leaps, but Robin leaped the first –
Ah, Pussy, of the Sand,
The Hopes so juicy ripening –
You almost bathed your Tongue –
When Bliss disclosed a hundred Toes –
And fled with every one –

Emily Dickinson

The chipmunk

My friends all know that I am shy,
But the chipmunk is twice as shy as I.
He moves with flickering indecision
Like stripes across the television.
He's like the shadow of a cloud,
Or Emily Dickinson read aloud.

Ogden Nash

The voice of the lobster

"'Tis the voice of the Lobster," I hear him declare
"You have baked me too brown, I must sugar my hair."
As a duck with its eyelids, so he with his nose
Trims his belt and his buttons, and turns out his toes.
When the sands are all dry, he is gay as a lark,
And will talk in contemptuous terms of the Shark;
But when the tide rises and sharks are around;
His voice has a timid and tremulous sound.

"I passed by his garden, and marked, with one eye
How the Owl and the Panther were sharing a pie,
The Panther took pie-crust, and gravy, and meat,
While the Owl had the dish as its share of the treat.
When the pie was all finished, the Owl, as a boon,
Was kindly permitted to pocket the spoon;
While the Panther received knife and fork with a growl,
And concluded the banquet by eating —"

Lewis Carroll

Bees

You voluble,
Velvety
Vehement fellows
That play on your
Flying and
Musical cellos,
All goldenly
Girdled you
Serenade clover,
Each artist in
Bass but a
Bibulous rover!

You passionate,
Powdery
Pastoral bandits,
Who gave you your
Roaming and
Rollicking mandates?
Come out of my
Foxglove; come
Out of my roses
You bees with the
Plushy and
Plausible noses!

Norman Rowland Gale

Flames

Smokey the Bear heads
into the autumn woods
with a red can of gasoline
and a box of wooden matches.
His ranger's hat is cocked
at a disturbing angle.
His brown fur gleams
under the high sun
as his paws, the size
of catcher's mitts,
crackle into the distance.
He is sick of dispensing
warnings to the careless,
the half-wit camper,
the dumbbell hiker.
He is going to show them
how a professional does it.

Billy Collins

The spangled pandemonium

The spangled pandemonium
Is missing from the zoo.
He bent the bars the barest bit,
And slithered glibly through.

He crawled across the moated wall,
He climbed the mango tree,
And when the keeper scrambled up,
He nipped him in the knee.

To all of you a warning
Not to wander after dark,
Or if you must, make very sure
You stay out of the park.

For the spangled pandemonium
Is missing from the zoo,
And since he nipped his keeper,
He would just as soon nip you!

Palmer Brown

The great panjandrum

So she went into the garden
to cut a cabbage-leaf
to make an apple-pie;
and at the same time
a great she-bear, coming down the street,
pops its head into the shop.
What! no soap?
    So he died,
and she very imprudently married the Barber:
and there were present
the Picninnies,
        and the Joblillies,
            and the Garyulies,
and the great Panjandrum himself,
with the little round button at top;
and they all fell to playing the game of catch-as-catch-can,
till the gunpowder ran out at the heels of their boots

Samuel Foote

Freedom quarter

I put my cap in the cage
and went out with the bird on my head
So
one no longer salutes
asked the commanding officer
No
one no longer salutes
replied the bird
Ah good
excuse me I thought one saluted
said the commanding officer
You are fully excused everybody makes mistakes
said the bird

Jacques Prévert
(Translated from the French by Lawrence Ferlinghetti)

Haiku

Now listen, you watermelons –
if any thieves come –
turn into frogs!

Issa
(Translated fom the Japanese by Robert Bly)

Toast to appetite

I intend to eat the bear
That you see over there.

My dog would like to eat it, but
I have too well trained the mutt.

The bear is mine.
First, some wine,

Then I'm going to eat the bear.
Broiled, mostly, medium rare.

Eat it all, from zotch to goozle.
Small bits fried in lard, as usual.

May well eat it all tonight.
Couldn't, without Appetite.

Appetite! Every bite

I take I owe to you for being there.
And now, I'll be off with my bear.

Roy Blount, Jr.

The embarrassing episode
of little miss muffet

Little Miss Muffet discovered a tuffet,
(Which never occurred to the rest of us)
And, as 'twas a June day, and just about noonday,
She wanted to eat – like the best of us:
Her diet was whey, and I hasten to say
It is wholesome and people grow fat on it.
The spot being lonely, the lady not only
Discovered the tuffet, but sat on it.

A rivulet gabbled beside her and babbled,
As rivulets always are thought to do,
And dragon flies sported around and cavorted,
As poets say dragon flies ought to do;
When, glancing aside for a moment, she spied
A horrible sight that brought fear to her,
A hideous spider was sitting beside her,
And most unavoidably near to her!

Albeit unsightly, this creature politely Said:
"Madam, I earnestly vow to you,
I'm penitent that I did not bring my hat.
I Should otherwise certainly bow to you."
Though anxious to please, he was so ill at ease
That he lost all his sense of propriety,
And grew so inept that he clumsily stept
In her plate – which is barred in Society.

This curious error completed her terror;
She shuddered, and growing much paler, not
Only left tuffet, but dealt him a buffet
Which doubled him up in a sailor knot.
It should be explained that at this he was pained:
He cried: "I have vexed you, no doubt of it!
Your fist's like a truncheon." "You're still in my luncheon,"
Was all that she answered. "Get out of it!"

And the Moral is this: Be it madam or miss
To whom you have something to say,
You are only absurd when you get in the curd
But you're rude when you get in the whey.

Guy Wetmore Carryl

The universal favorite

Salad of greens! Salad of greens!
What's that? You like it? Go tell the Marines!
Greenery yellery, lettuce and celery,
How I abominate salad of greens!
Romaine and escarole, cress, and tomatoes,
Radishes, chicory, beets, and potatoes;
Apples and cabbages, seeded white grapes,
Peppers and onions and chervil and cepes.
Yes, in the best of our modern cuisines,
They serve you that terrible salad of greens!
Capers and olives, mustard and chilli,
Cucumbers, artichokes, chives, piccalilli.
Pickles, paprika, pimentos, and cheese
Tips of asparagus, carrots and peas.
Cantaloupe, cherries, grapefruit, nectarines,
Dock, avocado, and haricot beans;
Oh, Fate, let me fly to some far distant scenes,
In villages, hamlets, or deserts or denes,
I care not if peopled by peasants or queens
If they never have heard of a Salad of Greens!
That very detestable
Horrid Comestible
Incredible
Inedible
Salad of Greens

Carolyn Wells

Recipe for a salad

To make this condiment your poet begs
The pounded yellow of two hard-boil'd eggs;
Two boiled potatoes, passed through kitchen seive,
Smoothness and softness to the salad give.
Let onion atoms lurk within the bowl,
And, half-suspected, animate the whole.
Of mordant mustard add a single spoon,
Distrust the condiment that bites so soon;
But deem it not, thou man of herbs, a fault
To add a double quantity of salt;
Four times the spoon with oil of Lucca crown,
And twice with vinegar procur'd from town;
And lastly o'er the flavor'd compound toss
A magic soupçon of anchovy sauce.
Oh, green and glorious! Oh, herbaceous treat!
Twould tempt the dying anchorite to eat;
Back to the world he'd turn his fleeting soul,
And plunge his fingers in the salad-bowl!
Serenely full, the epicure would say,
'Fate cannot harm me, I have dined today.'

Sydney Smith

Beautiful soup

Beautiful Soup, so rich and green,
Waiting in a hot tureen!
Who for such dainties would not stoop?
Soup of the evening, beautiful Soup!
Soup of the evening, beautiful Soup!

Beau—ootiful Soo-oop! Beau—ootiful Soo-oop! Soo—oop
of the e—e—evening,
     Beautiful, beautiful Soup!

Beautiful Soup! Who cares for fish,
Game, or any other dish?
Who would not give all else for two
Pennyworth only of Beautiful Soup?
Pennyworth only of beautiful Soup?

Beau—ootiful Soo-oop! Beau—ootiful Soo-oop! Soo—oop
of the e—e—evening,
     Beautiful, beauti—FUL SOUP!

Lewis Carroll

Rice pudding

What is the matter with Mary Jane?
She's crying with all her might and main,
And she won't eat her dinner – rice pudding again –
What is the matter with Mary Jane?
What is the matter with Mary Jane?
I've promised her dolls and a daisy-chain,
And a book about animals – all in vain –
What is the matter with Mary Jane?
What is the matter with Mary Jane?
She's perfectly well, and she hasn't a pain;
But, look at her, now she's beginning again! –
What is the matter with Mary Jane?
What is the matter with Mary Jane?
I've promised her sweets and a ride in the train,
And I've begged her to stop for a bit and explain –
What is the matter with Mary Jane?
What is the matter with Mary Jane?
She's perfectly well and she hasn't a pain,
And it's lovely rice pudding for dinner again!
What is the matter with Mary Jane?

A.A. Milne

Bleezer's ice cream

I am Ebenezer Bleezer,
I run BLEEZER'S ICE CREAM STORE,
there are flavors in my freezer
you have never seen before,
twenty-eight divine creations
too delicious to resist,
why not do yourself a favor,
try the flavors on my list:

COCOA MOCHA MACARONI
TAPIOCA SMOKED BALONEY
CHECKERBERRY CHEDDAR CHEW
CHICKEN CHERRY HONEYDEW
TUTTI-FRUTTI STEWED TOMATO
TUNA TACO BAKED POTATO
LOBSTER LITCHI LIMA BEAN
MOZZARELLA MANGOSTEEN
ALMOND HAM MERINGUE SALAMI
YAM ANCHOVY PRUNE PASTRAMI
SASSAFRAS SOUVLAKI HASH
SUKIYAKI SUCCOTASH
BUTTER BRICKLE PEPPER PICKLE
POMEGRANATE PUMPERNICKEL
PEACH PIMENTO PIZZA PLUM
PEANUT PUMPKIN BUBBLEGUM
BROCCOLI BANANA BLUSTER
CHOCOLATE CHOP SUEY CLUSTER
AVOCADO BRUSSELS SPROUT

PERIWINKLE SAUERKRAUT
COTTON CANDY CARROT CUSTARD
CAULIFLOWER COLA MUSTARD
ONION DUMPLING DOUBLE DIP
TURNIP TRUFFLE TRIPLE FLIP
GARLIC GUMBO GRAVY GUAVA
LENTIL LEMON LIVER LAVA
ORANGE OLIVE BAGEL BEET
WATERMELON WAFFLE WHEAT

I am Ebenezer Bleezer,
I run BLEEZER'S ICE CREAM STORE,
taste a flavor from my freezer,
you will surely ask for more.

Jack Prelutsky

Song of the pancake man

I'm the pancake man,
And I do, when I can,
Eat pancakes by the score;
I bake them brown,
And swallow them down,
And loudly call for more.

I'll lay my stakes
That a million cakes
I can eat between two naps;
Then call for more,
A million and four,
Or a million and five, perhaps.

It makes me fat,
And more than that,
I'm jolly through and through;
I've been known to laugh
For a year and a half,
Or why not call it two

Oh, I long for a cake
As big as they make,
Say, fifty townships wide;
I would handle it quite
At a single bite
And stow it away inside.

John Edward Everett

A drink with something in it

There is something about a Martini,
A tingle remarkably pleasant;
A yellow, a mellow Martini;
I wish I had one at present.
There is something about a Martini,
Ere the dining and dancing begin,
And to tell you the truth,
It is not the vermouth –
I think that perhaps it's the gin.

Ogden Nash

Lines on the Mermaid Tavern

Souls of Poets dead and gone,
What Elysium have ye known,
Happy field or mossy cavern,
Choicer than the Mermaid Tavern?
Have ye tippled drink more fine
Than mine host's Canary wine?
Or are fruits of Paradise
Sweeter than those dainty pies
Of venison? O generous food!
Drest as though bold Robin Hood
Would, with his maid Marian,
Sup and bowse from horn and can.

I have heard that on a day
Mine host's sign-board flew away,
Nobody knew whither, till
An astrologer's old quill
To a sheepskin gave the story,
Said he saw you in your glory,
Underneath a new old sign
Sipping beverage divine,
And pledging with contented smack
The Mermaid in the Zodiac.

Souls of Poets dead and gone,
What Elysium have ye known,
Happy field or mossy cavern,
Choicer than the Mermaid Tavern?

John Keats

R-E-M-O-R-S-E

The cocktail is a pleasant drink,
It's mild and harmless, I don't think!
When you've had one, you call for two,
And then you don't care what you do!
Last night I hoisted twenty-three
Of those arrangements into me;
My wealth increased, I swelled with pride;
I was pickled, primed, and ossified.
R-e-m-o-r-s-e!

Those dry martinis were too much for me.
Last night at twelve I felt immense;
To day I feel like thirty cents.
At four I sought my whirling bed,
At eight I woke with such a head
it is no time for mirth or laughter –
The cold, gray dawn of the morning after.

If ever I want to sign the pledge,
It's the morning after I've had an edge;
When I've been full of the oil of joy
And fancied I was a sporty boy.
This world was one kaleidescope
Of purple bliss, transcendent hope.
But now I'm feeling mighty blue –
Three cheers for the W.C.T.U.!
R-e-m-o-r-s-e!

The water wagon is the place for me;
I think that somewhere in the game,
I wept and told my maiden name.
My eyes are bleared, my coppers hot;
I try to eat but I can not;
It is no time for mirth and laughter –
The cold, gray dawn of the morning after.

George Ade

The Irish pig

'Twas an evening in November,
As I very well remember,
I was strolling down the street in drunken pride,
But my knees were all aflutter,
So I landed in the gutter,
And a pig came up and lay down by my side.

Yes I lay there in the gutter
Thinking thoughts I could not utter,
When a colleen passing by did softly say,
"Ye can tell a man that boozes
By the company he chooses" –
At that the pig got up and walked away

Anonymous

The objection to being stepped on

At the end of the row
I stepped on the toe
Of an unemployed hoe.
It rose in offense
And struck me a blow
In the seat of my sense.
It wasn't to blame
But I called it a name.
And I must say it dealt
Me a blow that I felt
Like a malice prepense.
You may call me a fool,
But was there a rule
The weapon should be
Turned into a tool?
And what do we see?
The first tool I step on
Turned into a weapon.

Robert Frost

Pls, stop sendg

Pls, stop sendg msgs2ths
no, i am not linda,
I hv not slept w/yr sis,
+i wd nvr call any1's ma a slag.
Gd luk w/viag.
Luv, yr wrong no. xxx

Charlotte Fortune

Twelve things I don't want to hear

Assemble this in eight straightforward steps.
Start with a fish stock, made the day before.
The driver has arrived but sadly, drunk.
We'll need some disinfectant for the floor.
Ensure all surfaces are clean and dry.
There's been a problem, Madam, I'm afraid!
We'd better have the manhole cover up.
Apologies, the doctor's been delayed.
I'd love to bring a friend, he's so depressed.
They've put you on the camp bed in the hall.
There's just one table left, perhaps you'd share?
I know it's midnight, but I had to call…

Connie Bensley

Ballade of indignation

"I'm driving through New Mexico, let's say,
facing the glories of the setting sun.
But just before I get to Sante Fe
there you are, stranger, with your ganglion
sized brain and SUV that weighs a ton,
paying no mind to sunset's golden crown,
but nitter-nattering ninety-nine to one...
So would you kindly put your cell phone down?

I'm dining out, which is the perfect way
to make the brain cells sing in unison,
relaxing with my Merlot and filet,
when there you are with that damn cell phone on
your ear, discussing how some game's been won
and whether stocks are up or upside-down.
You're sharing all your life with everyone,
so would you kindly put your cell phone down?

Haven't you noticed it's a lovely day?
The kind that makes you want to jump and run?
But even jogging you can't throw away
that cell phone, can you? Why, you've just begun
to give your boss a sales plan that will stun
competitors and make your rivals drown.
Look out, you fool, you're running down a nun,
so would you kindly put your cell phone down?

L'Envoi

Friend, I'm no longer saying this for fun.
Road rage has made me rampage though the town.
I'm out of Prozac and I have a gun.
So would you kindly put your cell phone down?

Gail White

To people I hear talking loudly on their cell phones

It is VERY IMPORTANT
to take care of your cell phone!
Do you know how?

The best way is to drop it in
a deep pot of chicken fat
and bring to a boil.
Simmer for two hours.
Let cool.

James Stevenson

The perils of modern living

Well up above the tropostrata
There is a region stark and stellar
Where, on a streak of anti-matter
Lived Dr. Edward Anti-Teller.

Remote from Fusion's origin,
He lived unguessed and unawares
With all his antikith and kin,
And kept macassars on his chairs.

One morning, idling by the sea,
He spied a tin of monstrous girth
That bore three letters: A. E. C.
Out stepped a visitor from Earth.

Then, shouting gladly o'er the sands,
Met two who in their alien ways
Were like as lentils. Their right hands
Clasped, and the rest was gamma rays.

Harold P. Furth

Endangered species

The resins used to make products permanently
wrinkle-resistant invade the very structure of the cotton...
from an advertisement

No crumpling from a drawer then,
or creases from a crowded closet,
not even a hanger's shoulder marks,

and picture meeting on the street
a worn summer suit or dress
like a blank expression on a face:

none of those sit-stripes on our laps,
or pleats up and down our sleeves
flexing like an accordion.

And what about the nervous tucks
a hand leaves in a handkerchief
or the long day's corrugations in our socks?

Just look – the way your shirt sprawls now
on the bedroom floor, loose folds
like a lowered sail,

and the denim pool you're wading,
one foot, then the other stepping
from its ripples.

Think of the loss. No matter what we did,
our sheets and pillowcases
smooth as ice – after as before.

Jane O. Wayne

"Weather"

Once I dipt into the future far as human eye could see,
And I saw the Chief Forecaster, dead as any one can be –
Dead and damned and shut in Hades as a liar from his
    birth,
With a record of unreason seldome paralleled on earth.
While I looked he reared him solemnly, that incandescent
    youth,
From the coals that he'd preferred to the advantages of
    truth.
He cast his eyes about him and above him; then he wrote
On a slab of thin asbestos what I venture here to quote –
For I read it in the rose-light of the everlasting glow:
"Cloudy; variable winds, with local showers; cooler; snow."

Ambrose Bierce

Spring, etc.

And now at last I come to it: spring,
Spring with his shoures sote,
Shoures snowe stille in Minnesota
But spring all the same, starting all over
All of those worthy projects in grass and clover
That somehow got tabled last October.

Spring in the trees and gardens, spring in the mind,
Spring in the fields and rivers, spring in the blood,
Spring, spring, spring, and then again spring,
We, warm, bright, green, good.

So now at last I come to it,
Long long overdue,
Come to it late by bobsled and skate, but come
To it, by golly and gum!
To it! Tu-whit, tu-who!

Reed Whittemore

Either way

Isotherms and isobars,
Little whirligigs and jars –
Things like that I can't deny
This poor brain can mystify.
Yet I'm strong for all the chaps
Who devise those squiggly maps,
For you must admit the guess
Tallies rather more than less,
And when they prognosticate,
I for one, will freely state
That it's grand when they declare
Simply "Moderate and Fair."
Yep, I get a keen delight
When the weatherman is right.

Isobars and isotherms –
Those are pretty hefty terms.
Pressures, fronts and anything
Of the sort could never ring
Any mental bell for me,
Dumb-bell I in ology.
So when sages aren't too sharp
Do I slyly sniff and carp?
If they say it's going to go
Maybe down to ten below
And I wake at twenty-plus,
Do I fume and do I fuss?

Nope! I placidly infer
Man is often prone to err –
Life can seem a grand, sweet song
When the weatherman is wrong!

Anonymous

No!

No sun—no moon!
No morn—no noon!
No dawn—no dusk—no proper time of day—
No sky—no earthly view—
No distance looking blue—
No road—no street—no "t'other side this way"—
No end to any Row—
No indications where the Crescents go—
No top to any steeple—
No recognitions of familiar people—
No courtesies for showing 'em—
No knowing 'em!
No traveling at all—no locomotion—
No inkling of the way—no notion—
"No go" by land or ocean—
No mail—no post—
No news from any foreign coast—
No Park, no Ring, no afternoon gentility—
No company—no nobility—
No warmth, no cheerfulness, no healthful ease,
No comfortable feel in any member—
No shade, no shine, no butterflies, no bees,
No fruits, no flowers, no leaves, no birds—
November!

Thomas Hood

English weather

January's grey and slushy,
February's drim and drear,
March is wild and wet and windy,
April seldom brings much cheer.
In May a day or two of sunshine,
Three or four in June, perhaps.
July is usually filthy,
August skies are open taps.
In September things start dying,
Then comes cold October mist.
November we make plans to spend
The best part of December pissed.

Wendy Cope

The devil in Texas

He scattered tarantulas over the roads,
Put thorns on the cactus and horns on the toads,
He sprinkled the sands with millions of ants
So the man that sits down must wear soles on his pants.
He lengthened the horns of the Texas steer,
And added an inch to the jack rabbit's ear;
He put water puppies in all of the lakes,
And under the rocks he put rattlesnakes.

He hung thorns and brambles on all of the trees,
He mixed up the dust with jiggers and fleas;
The rattlesnake bites you, the scorpion stings,
The mosquito delights you by buzzing his wings.
The heat in the summer's a hundred and ten,
Too hot for the Devil and too hot for men;
And all who remained in that climate soon bore
Cuts, bites, stings, and scratches, and blisters galore.

Anonymous

Selecting a reader

First, I would have her be beautiful,
and walking carefully up on my poetry
at the loneliest moment of an afternoon,
her hair still damp at the neck
from washing it. She should be wearing
a raincoat, an old one, dirty
from not having money enough for the cleaners.
She will take out her glasses, and there
in the bookstore, she will thumb
over my poems, then put the book back
up on its shelf. She will say to herself,
"For that kind of money, I can get
my raincoat cleaned." And she will.

Ted Kooser

Eating poetry

Ink runs from the corners of my mouth.
There is no happiness like mine.
I have been eating poetry.

The librarian does not believe what she sees.
Her eyes are sad
and she walks with her hands in her dress.

The poems are gone.
The light is dim.
The dogs are on the basement stairs and coming up.

Their eyeballs roll,
their blond legs burn like brush.
The poor librarian begins to stamp her feet and weep.

She does not understand.
When I get on my knees and lick her hand,
she screams.

I am a new man.
I snarl at her and bark.
I romp with joy in the bookish dark.

Mark Strand

I'm nobody! who are you?

I'm Nobody! Who are you?
Are you – Nobody – too?
Then there's a pair of us?
Don't tell! they'd advertise – you know!

How dreary – to be – Somebody!
How public – like a Frog –
To tell one's name – the livelong June –
To an admiring Bog!

Emily Dickinson

96 Vandam

I am going to carry my bed into New York City tonight
complete with dangling sheets and ripped blankets;
I am going to push it across three dark highways
or coast along under 600,000 faint stars.
I want to have it with me so I don't have to beg
for too much shelter from my weak and exhausted friends.
I want to be as close as possible to my pillow
in case a dream or a fantasy should pass by.
I want to fall asleep on my own fire escape
and wake up dazed and hungry
to the sound of garbage grinding in the street below
and the smell of coffee cooking in the window above.

Gerald Stern

The bagel

I stopped to pick up the bagel
rolling away in the wind,
annoyed with myself
for having dropped it
as if it were a portent.
Faster and faster it rolled,
with me running after it
bent low, gritting my teeth,
and I found myself doubled over
and rolling down the street
head over heels, one complete somersault
after another like a bagel
and strangely happy with myself.

David Ignatow

Poem (Lana Turner has collapsed!)

Lana Turner has collapsed!
I was trotting along and suddenly
it started raining and snowing
and you said it was hailing
but hailing hits you on the head
hard so it was really snowing and
raining and I was in such a hurry
to meet you but the traffic
was acting exactly like the sky
and suddenly I see a headline
LANA TURNER HAS COLLAPSED!
there is no snow in Hollywood
there is no rain in California
I have been to lots of parties
and acted perfectly disgraceful
but I never actually collapsed
oh Lana Turner we love you get up

Frank O'Hara

Advice from the experts

      I lay down in the empty street and parked
My feet against the gutter's curb while from
The building above a bunch of gawkers perched
Along its ledges urged me don't, don't jump.

Bill Knott

Social security

No one is safe. The streets are unsafe.
Even in the safety zones, it's not safe.
Even safe sex is not safe.
Even things you lock up in a safe
are not safe. Never deposit anything
in a safe-deposit box, because it
won't be safe there. Nobody is safe
at home during baseball games anymore.

At night I go around in the dark
locking everything, returning
a few minutes later
to make sure I locked
everything. It's not safe here.
It's not safe and they know it.
People get hurt using safety pins.

It was not always this way.
Long ago, everyone felt safe. Aristotle
never felt danger. Herodotus felt danger
only when Xerxes was around. Young women
were afraid of wingèd dragons, but felt
relaxed otherwise. Timotheus, however,

was terrified of storms until he played
one on the flute. After that, everyone
was more afraid of him than of the violent
west wind, which was fine with Timotheus.
Euclid, full of music himself, believed only
that there was safety in numbers.

Terence Winch

Waving at trains

Do people who wave at trains
Wave at the driver, or at the train itself?
Or, do people who wave at trains
Wave at the passengers? Those hurtling strangers,
The unidentifiable flying faces?

They must think we like being waved at.
Children do perhaps, and alone
In a compartment, the occasional passenger
Who is himself a secret waver at trains.
But most of us are unimpressed.

Some even think they're daft.
Stuck out there in a field, grinning.
But our ignoring them, our blank faces,
Even our pulled tongues and up you signs
Come three miles further down the line.

Out of harm's way by then
They continue their walk.
Refreshed and made pure, by the mistaken belief
That their love has been returned,
Because they have not seen it rejected.

It's like God in a way. Another day
Another universe. Always off somewhere.
And left behind, the faithful few,
Stuck out there. Not a care in the world.
All innocence. Arms in the air. Waving.

Roger McGough

Delayed action

Korf invents some jokes of a new sort
That only many hours later work.
Everybody listens to them, bored.

Yet, like some still fuse glowing in the dark,
You wake up suddenly that night in bed
Beaming like a baby newly fed.

Christian Morgenstern
(Translated from the German by W. D. Snodgrass and Lore Segal)

The young pobble's guide to his toes

Everything comes, everything goes.
Some day you must say goodbye to your toes—
all bitten off by the beasts of the sea
or fading away by a gradual degree,
vanishing into an elbowless night
All blurred and dim in your elderly sight.
The sun goes down and the eye gives up,
your toes will fade, kerflip, kerflup…

The moral shines bright as a mermaid's hair.
Count them and keep them while they're still there!

Gavin Ewart

The limitations of youth

I'd like to be a cowboy an' ride a fiery hoss
Way out into the big an' boundless west;
I'd kill the bears an' catamounts an' wolves I come across,
An' I'd pluck the bal' head eagle from his nest!
With my pistols at my side,
I would roam the prairers wide,
An' to scalp the savage Injun in his wigwam would I
    ride –
If I darst; but I darsen't!
I'd like to go to Afriky an' hunt the lions there,
An' the biggest ollyfunts you ever saw!
I would track the fierce gorilla to his equatorial lair,
An' beard the cannybull that eats folks raw!
I'd chase the pizen snakes
An' the 'pottimus that makes
His nest down at the bottom of unfathomable lakes –
If I darst; but I darsen't!
I would I were a pirut to sail the ocean blue,
With a big black flag aflyin' overhead;
I would scour the billowy main with my gallant pirut crew
An' dye the sea a gouty, gory red!
With my cutlass in my hand
On the quarterdeck I'd stand
And to deeds of heroism I'd incite my pirut band –
If I darst; but I darsen't!
And, if I darst, I'd lick my pa for the times that he's licked
me!

I'd lick my brother an' my teacher, too!
I'd lick the fellers that call round on sister after tea,
An' I'd keep on lickin' folks till I got through!
You bet! I'd run away
From my lessons to my play,
An' I'd shoo the hens, an' tease the cat, an' kiss the girls all
        day –
If I darst; but I darsen't!

Eugene Field

Mind body problem

When I think of my youth I feel sorry not for myself
but for my body. It was so direct
and simple, so rational in its desires,
wanting to be touched the way an otter
loves water, the way a giraffe
wants to amble the edge of the forest, nuzzling
the tender leaves at the tips of the trees. It seems
unfair, somehow, that my body had to suffer
because I, by which I mean my mind, was saddled
with certain unfortunate high-minded romantic notions
that made me tyrannize and patronize it
like a cruel medieval baron, or an ambitious
English-professor husband ashamed of his wife –
her love of sad movies, her budget casseroles
and regional vowels. Perhaps
my body would have liked to make some of our dates,
to come home at four in the morning and answer my
     scowl
with "None of your business!" Perhaps
it would have liked more presents: silks, mascaras.
If we had had a more democratic arrangement
we might even have come, despite our different
backgrounds,

to a grudging respect for each other, like Tony Curtis
and Sidney Poitie handcuffed together
instead of the current curious shift of power
in which I feel I am being reluctantly
dragged along my body as though by some
swift and powerful dog. How eagerly
it plunges ahead, not stopping for anything,
as though it knows exactly where we are going.

Katha Pollitt

Peekabo, I almost see you

Middle-aged life is merry, and I love to
lead it,
But there comes a day when your eyes
are all right but your arm isn't long
enough
to hold the telephone book where you can read it,
And your friends get jocular, so you go
to the oculist,
And of all your friends he is the joculist,
So over his facetiousness let us skim,
Only noting that he has been waiting for you ever since
you said Good evening to his grandfather clock under
the impression that it was him,
And you look at his chart and it says SHRDLU
    QWERTYOP,
and you say Well, why SHRDNTLU QWERTYOP? and
he says one set of glasses won't do.
You need two.
One for reading Erle Stanley Gardner's Perry Mason and
Keats's "Endymion" with,
And the other for walking around without saying Hello
to strange wymion with.
So you spend your time taking off your seeing glasses to
    put
on your reading glasses, and then remembering that your
reading glasses are upstairs or in the car,

And then you can't find your seeing glasses again because
without them on you can't see where they are.
Enough of such mishaps, they would try the patience of an
    ox,
I prefer to forget both pairs of glasses and pass my
    declining
years saluting strange women and grandfather clocks.

Ogden Nash

Warning

When I am an old woman I shall wear purple
With a red hat which doesn't go, and doesn't suit me.
And I shall spend my pension on brandy and summer
    gloves
And satin sandals, and say we've no money for butter.
I shall sit down on the pavement when I'm tired
And gobble up samples in shops and press alarm bells
And run my stick along the public railings
And make up for the sobriety of my youth.
I shall go out in my slippers in the rain
And pick the flowers in other people's gardens
And learn to spit.

You can wear terrible shirts and grow more fat
And eat three pounds of sausages at a go
Or only bread and pickle for a week
And hoard pens and pencils and beermats and things in
    boxes.

But now we must have clothes that keep us dry
And pay our rent and not swear in the street
And set a good example for the children.
We must have friends to dinner and read the papers.

But maybe I ought to practice a little now?
So people who know me are not too shocked and surprised
When suddenly I am old, and start to wear purple.

Jenny Joseph

The little old lady in lavender silk

I was seventy-seven, come August,
    I shall shortly be losing my bloom;
I've experienced zephyr and raw gust
    And (symbolical) flood and simoom.

When you come to this time of abatement,
    To this passing from Summer to Fall,
It is manners to issue a statement
    As to what you got out of it all.

So I'll say, though reflection unnerves me
    And pronouncements I dodge as I can,
That I think (if my memory serves me)
    There was nothing more fun than a man!

In my youth, when the crescent was too wan
    To embarrass with beams from above,
By the aid of some local Don Juan
    I fell into the habit of love.

And I learned how to kiss and be merry – an
    Education left better unsung.
My neglect of the waters Pierian
    Was a scandal, when Grandma was young.

Though the shabby unbalanced the splendid,
    And the bitter outmeasured the sweet,

I should certainly do as I then did,
    Were I given the chance to repeat.

For contrition is hollow and wraithful,
    And regret is no part of my plan,
And I think (if my memory's faithful)
    There was nothing more fun than a man!

Dorothy Parker

maggie and milly and molly and may

maggie and milly and molly and may
went down to the beach (to play one day)
and maggie discovered a shell that sang
so sweetly she couldn't remember her troubles, and
milly befriended a stranded star
whose rays five languid fingers were;
and molly was chased by a horrible thing
which raced sideways while blowing bubbles:and
may came home with a smooth round stone
as small as a world and as large as alone.
For whatever we lose (like a you or a me)
it's always ourselves we find in the sea

e. e. cummings

Advice to young children

"Children who paddle where the ocean bed shelves steeply
Must take great care they do not,
Paddle too deeply."

Thus spake the awful aging couple
Whose hearts the years had turned to rubble.

But the little children, to save any bother,
Let it in one year and out at the other.

Stevie Smith

Athena

My temples throb, my pulses boil
I'm sick of Song, and Ode, and Ballad –
So, Thyrsis, take the Midnight Oil
And pour it on a lobster salad.
My brain is dull, my sight is foul,
I cannot write a verse, or read –
Then, Pallas, take away thine Owl,
And let us have a Lark instead.

Thomas Hood

God says yes to me

I asked God if it was okay to be melodramatic
and she said yes
I asked her if it was okay to be short
and she said it sure is
I asked her if I could wear nail polish
or not wear nail polish
and she said honey
she calls me that sometimes
she said you can do just exactly
what you want to
Thanks God I said
And is it even okay if I don't paragraph
my letters
Sweetcakes God said
who knows where she picked that up
what I'm telling you is
Yes Yes Yes

Kaylin Haught

I didn't go to church today

I didn't go to church today,
I trust the Lord to understand.
The surf was swirling blue and white,
The children swirling on the sand.
He knows, He knows how brief my stay,
How brief this spell of summer weather,
He knows when I am said and done
We'll have plenty of time together.

Ogden Nash

Listening to jazz now

1.

Listening to jazz now, I'm happy
       sun shining outside like it was my lifetime
achievement award.
                    I'm happy,
with my friend and her dog up in Durango, her emailing
       me this morning
no coon hound ailing yowls
vibrant I love yous.
              I'm happy,
       my smile a big Monarch butterfly
          after having juiced up some carrots, garlic,
    seaweed,
      I stroll the riverbank, lazy as a deep cello
in a basement bar—

                    smoke, cagney'd out patrons
                    caramcl and chocolate women in black
                         shoulder strap satin dresses,
                    and red high heels.

Jimmy Santiago Baca

Happiness is being Danish

says the license plate frame
of the sky blue compact
in front of me at the stop light,
and I think, well, what chance
did I have, with parents like mine –
French, and Irish, and German –
and under the harangue
of the windshield wipers,
I can just make out the sighs
of my unhappy chromosomes,
forced to perform their slow minuet
in green tights, to the strains
of martial music.

And these others
waiting at the intersection,
I'll bet they're not Danish either
and never will be – exiles, all of us,
behind the razor wire of "Being,"
a state which precludes becoming,
by act of will, or the usual consular
channels; required to declare
Either/Or when we yearn to settle
freely in Both/And; a dilemma
understood by no one

better than Kierkegaard,
saddest of Danes. See how he labors
in line behind us, alone
with the problem of Being,
weighing it over and over
in the long red light of sacrifice,
looking up now and then
from his notebook
to remember Regine –

how they'd once danced the Hopsa
in the Town Hall Square,
then stood, hand in hand,
in the unequivocal light
of the Copenhagen winter, happy
to be Danish and in love,
with blue sky ahead of them,
waiting for green.

Jennifer Maier

Happiness

I asked the professors who teach the meaning of life to tell
    me what is happiness.
And I went to famous executives who boss the work of
    thousands of men.
They all shook their heads and gave me a smile as though
    I was trying to fool with them
And then one Sunday afternoon I wandered out along
    the Desplaines river
And I saw a crowd of Hungarians under the trees with
    their women and children and a keg of beer and an
    accordion.

Carl Sandburg

Summer haiku

All night the peepers
Singing around our small pond,
Drunk men, happy men.

A mother bat soars
Crazily across the moon,
Mouth full of insects.

A grasshopper leaps
Through the meadow, escaping
The mower. This time.

I am so little,
Thinks the leaping grasshopper,
Why not let me live?

Alicia Ostriker

Astro-gymnastics

Do-it-yourself grook

Go on a starlit night,
stand on your head,
leave your feet dangling
outwards into space,
and let the starry
firmament you tread
be, for the moment,
your elected base.

Feel Earth's colossal weight
of ice and granite,
of molten magma,
water, iron, and lead;
and briefly hold
this strangely solid planet
balanced upon
your strangely solid head.

Piet Hein
(Translated from the Belgian by the author)

Like Anne Shirley's house

I want a house that lifts itself
from the ground with a porch
like the lap of an apron
made to hold me in wicker.
The floor will be fir, clear
vertical grain; cut, milled,
shipped down from the north,
painted over each spring
semigloss gray-deck gray
it will say on the can.

People will come to a porch
composed around
the private dignity of a house
open to friends.

It will have corners for secrets.
The trellised west side
dripping rampant vine, flowering
frantic with bees in July,
a niche for the intimate glance
as amethyst deepens to violet
and the small wild loves of earth
sing out its rhythm
as if the whole country round
were gliding to bliss on rockers.

Faye George

Laughing Song

When the green woods laugh with the voice of joy,
And the dimpling stream runs laughing by;

When the air does laugh with our merry wit,
And the green hill laughs with the noise of it;

When the meadows laugh with lively green,
And the grasshopper laughs in the merry scene,

When Mary and Susan and Emily
With their sweet round mouths sing "Ha, ha he!"

When the painted birds laugh in the shade,
Where our table with cherries and nuts is spread:

Come live, and be merry, and join with me,
To sing the sweet chorus of "Ha, ha, he!"

William Blake

Index of first lines

Biographical notes

Kim Addonizio (1954–): Born in Washington D.C. Author of three books of poetry. Her latest collection, *What Is This Thing Called Love* was published in 2004. Addonizio currently teaches private poetry workshops in Oakland, California.

George Ade (1866–1944): Born in Kentland Indiana. Well known as a humorist and playwright, he also wrote light verse. Ade worked on Chicago newspapers before publishing his own work from 1896.

Jimmy Santiago Baca (1952–): Born in Santa Fe, New Mexico. Taught himself to read while in jail for drug possession. His poetry was published by Denise Levertov, and he went on to win many awards including the Pushcart Prize, the American Book Award, and the National Poetry Award. He has published seven poetry collections—the latest is *Winter Poems Along the Rio Grande* (2004).

Isabel Frances Bellows: A prolific light verse writer and humorist, she was a regular contributor to St Nicholas Magazine, an American publication for children that was published from 1873–1939. It published some of the best known American and English writers.

Connie Bensley (1929–) A wry, quirkily-humorous poet, she has published several poetry collections—her latest are *The Back and the Front Of It* (2000), *Choosing To Be a Swan* (1994) and *Central Reservations* (1990). She lives in London.

David Berman (1967–): Born in Williamsburg, Virginia. He is frontman for the popular indie rock band, the Silver Jews. Berman was educated at the University of Virginia, and the University of Massachusetts. He now lives in Nashville, Tennessee. His debut poetry collection *Open Air* was published in 2000 to widespread praise.

Ambrose Bierce (1842–1914): Born in Ohio. Noted for his sardonic, macabre tales, he was also a political satirist, journalist, columnist, and reviewer. The collections *A Vision of Doom* (1980) and *Poems of Ambrose Bierce* (1996) are good introductions to his poetry.

William Blake (1757–1827): Born in London. Poet and engraver, now world famous for his visionary works, Blake's genius was not widely recognized in his day.

Laurel Blossom (1943–): Born in Washington, DC. Her most recent book of poetry is *Wednesday: New and Selected* Poems (2004). Earlier books include *The Papers Said* (1993), *What's Wrong* (1987), and *Any Minute* (1979). Her work has appeared in a number of anthologies, and in national journals including *Poetry, The American Poetry Review, Pequod, The Paris Review, The Carolina Quarterly, Deadsnake Apotheosis, Many Mountains Moving*, and *Harper's Magazine*.

Roy Blount, Jr. (1941–): Born in Indianapolis. A popular humorist, journalist, sportswriter, poet, novelist, performer, editor, lyricist, lecturer, screenwriter, dramatist, and philologist. Blount has written in many forms, and is the author of 19 books and successful screenplays.

Rupert Brooke (1887–1915): Born in Warwickshire, England. At the outbreak of World War I he enlisted in the Royal Naval Division. His most famous work, the sonnet sequence *1914 and Other Poems*, appeared in 1915. Charming, cultivated, and witty, he became a legendary figure amongst the poets of the First World War.

John Bunyan (1628–1688): Born in Bedfordshire, England. He is most famous for his religious narratives *Pilgrim's Progress* and *Grace Abounding*. He was also a fine poet, and wrote much of his work while in prison for his non-conformist beliefs.

Lewis Carroll (1832–1898): Born in Cheshire, England. A gifted mathematician, he wrote the children's classic *Alice's Adventures in Wonderland* in 1865, followed by *Through the Looking Glass* in 1872. He is also famous for his 'nonsense' poetry, which demonstrates his highly imaginative wit.

Guy Wetmore Carryl (1873–1904): Born in New York City, Carryl was skilled at parodying nursery rhymes and children's stories in cynical, witty mode. *Fables for the Frivolous* (1898), and *Grimm Tales made Gay* (1902), are typical examples.

Lucille Clifton (1936–): Born in Depew, New York. *Blessing the Boats: New and Selected Poems*, won the National Book Award for Poetry in 2001. Other books include *The Terrible Stories* (1995), nominated for the National Book Award, *The Book of Light* (1993), *Quilting: Poems 1987–1990* (1991), *Good Woman: Poems and a Memoir 1969–1980* (1987), *Two-Headed Woman* (1980), winner of the University of Massachusetts Press Juniper Prize; and *An Ordinary Woman* (1974).

Billy Collins (1941–): Born in New York City. He is one of America's most popular poets. Collins's books include *Nine Horses* (2002), *Sailing Alone Around the Room: New and Selected Poems* (2001), *The Art of Drowning* (1995), and *Questions About Angels* (1991). A recent Poet Laureate of the United States, he was appointed New York State Poet Laureate 2004–2006.

Wendy Cope (1945–): Born in Erith, Kent. Widely popular British poet. After years spent teaching, Cope began writing full time in 1986. Her poetry collections include *Making Cocoa for Kingsley Amis* (1986), *Serious Concerns* (1992), and *If I Don't Know* (2001), which was shortlisted for the Whitbread Poetry Award. She lives in Winchester, England.

e. e. cummings (1894–1962): Born in Cambridge, Massachusetts. He used experimental poetic forms and punctuation, and is admired for the playful spirit of his poetry.

Anna Denise: American poet. Her poem 'How to Change a Frog into a Prince' is included in *The Poets' Grimm: 20th Century Poems from Grimm's Fairy Tales, 2003.*

Emily Dickinson (1830–1886): A giant presence in 19th-century American poetry, she lived as a virtual recluse at her home in Amherst, Massachusetts. Only seven of her poems were published in her lifetime— her work was collected and published after her death.

John Edward Everett: American poet born in Kansas. Author of *Quillings in Verse* (1912), a celebration of life in his home state.

Gavin Ewart (1916–1995): Born in London. A prominent figure of the 1930s London poetry scene, he was known for his wickedly comic light verse. His many poetry collections include *The Gavin Ewart Show* (1971), *Be My Guest!* (1975), *The Young Pobble's Guide to His Toes* (1985), and his *Selected Poems 1933–1993*, (1996).

Eugene Field (1850–1895): Born in St Louis, Missouri. He is unusual in that he only wrote poetry for children. Some of his most famous poems are 'Wynken, Blynken, and Nod'; 'The Duel'; and 'Little Boy Blue'.

Samuel Foote (1720–1777): English actor and playwright, he was famed for his wit and ability to mimic others. Foote's poem 'The Great Panjandrum' was composed in 1755 for the actor Charles Macklin.

Charlotte Fortune (1979–): The British poet is a former archaeology student at Liverpool University and was one of the prize winners of a recent 'text message' poetry competition run by *The Guardian* newspaper.

Robert Frost (1874–1963): Born in California, he spent most of his life in New England. Frost won the Pulitzer Prize for poetry four times, and read his poem 'The Gift Outright' at the inauguration of President John F Kennedy.

Harold P. Furth (1930–2002): Born in Vienna. Renowned astro-physicist and specialist in magnetic fusion energy. His poem 'The Perils of Modern Living' was published in *The New Yorker* in 1956, and demonstrated his great skill in composing light verse.

Norman Rowland Gale (1862–1942): English poet and author of over 50 collections of light verse including *Cricket Songs and Other Trifling Verses* (1890), *A Verdant Country* (1893), *On Two Strings* (1894), *The Country Muse* (1894), and *Song in September* (1912).

Faye George: A native of Weymouth Massachusetts, her poetry has won several awards including Arizona Poetry Society's Memorial Award, the New England Poetry Club's Gretchen Warren Award and the Erika Mumford Prize. She has published *A Wound on Stone* (2001), and *Back Roads* 2003.

Dana Gioia (1950–): Born in Los Angeles, California. Poet, critic, and best selling anthologist. His poems, translations, essays, and reviews have appeared in many magazines including *The New Yorker*, *The Atlantic*, *The Washington Post Book World*, *The New York Times Book Review*, *Slate*, and *The Hudson Review*. His poetry collections include *Daily Horoscope* (1986), *The Gods of Winter* (1991), and *Interrogations at Noon* (2001) which won him the American Book Award.

Beth Gylys (1964 –): Born in Passaic, New Jersey. Associate Professor at Georgia State University, her poetry has been published in *The Paris Review*, *The New Republic*, *The Boston Review*, *Ploughshares*, *Antioch Review*, *The Southern Review*, and many other literary magazines including *Wind*. Her book, *Bodies that Hum*, (1999) won the Gerald Cable Poetry Award, and her book *Balloon Heart* (1997) *won* The Quentin R. Howard Poetry Prize. Her latest book, *Spot in the Dark* was published in 2004.

Donald Hall (1928–): Born in New Haven, Connecticut. Hall served as poetry editor for *Paris Review*. Author of 15 books of poetry, and winner of many awards, he has taught at Stanford, Harvard, and the University of Michigan. He was married to fellow poet, the late Jane Kenyon. His recent collection *The Painted Bed* was published in 2002.

Kaylin Haught (1947–): Born in Albion, Illinois, she grew up in Oklahoma. Her poems have appeared in *ONTHEBUS, Being Alive,* and *Poetry 180*. Haught is currently working on her first book of poetry with the working title *Endangered Species*.

Piet Hein (1905–1996): Danish poet and scientist, his pen name was Kumbel. He called his witty, epigrammatic poems 'grooks.' They were illustrated with his own line drawings. Hein invented the geometric puzzle, the Soma Cube,

Elizabeth Holmes: Writer and editor living in Ithaca, New York. Her poems have appeared in *Poetry, The Gettysburg Review, Michigan Quarterly Review,* and other journals. Her first book, *The Patience of the Cloud Photographer,* was published in 1997 by Carnegie Mellon University Press.

Thomas Hood (1799–1845): Born in London. A poet well respected by his contemporaries, he is chiefly remembered for his comic verse, but was also author of more serious work. In 1829 he became editor of *The Gem,* and published works by Tennyson, among others.

David Ignatow (1914–1997): Born in New York City. He published 17 books, the last—*At My Ease: Uncollected Poems of the Fifties and Sixties* (1998)—posthumously. He was editor of various literary journals, and served as poet-in-residence and professor at a number of colleges and universities throughout the United States.

Kobayashi Issa (1763–1828): Born in Shinano Province, Japan. A gifted Haiku poet, he wrote personal, accessible poetry.

Jenny Joseph (1932–): Born in Birmingham, England, she is a well known British poet. Her first book of poems, *The Unlooked-for Season* (1960), won her a Gregory Award and she won a Cholmondeley Award for her second collection *Rose in the Afternoon* (1974). She also published *The Thinking Heart* (1978), and *Beyond Descartes* (1983). Her *Selected Poems* (1992) contains poems from all these books.

John Keats (1795–1821): Born in London. He died when he was 25, and had published only 54 poems. Considered to be one of the finest poets of all time, he is particularly admired for his sonnets and odes.

X. J. Kennedy (1929–): Born in Dover, New Jersey. His first collection of poetry *Nude Descending a Staircase* (1961) won the Lamont Poetry Selection. He has since won numerous other awards, and edited the *Paris Review*. His collection *Dark Horses: New Poems* was published in1992.

Galway Kinnell (1927–): Born in Rhode Island. He was awarded both the Pulitzer Prize for Poetry and the National Book Award for Poetry for his *Selected Poems* published in 2000. He is a visiting professor at New York University, but lives mostly in Vermont.

Bill Knott: Born in Carson City, Michigan. He is Associate Professor of Writing, Literature and Publishing at Emerson College in Boston. Knott is the author of nine books of poetry, and is featured in most major journals and poetry magazines. His book *Selected and Collected Poems* was the 1979 winner of the Elliston Prize. His collections include *Poems: 1963–1988* (1989), *Outremer* (1989), and *The Quicken Tree* (1995).

Ron Koertge: Born in Illinois. Poet, college professor, and an instructor in the MFA Writing for Children Program at Vermont College, Koertge's books for children have won him great accolades in the USA.

Ted Kooser (1939–): Born in Ames, Iowa. Currently Poet Laureate of the United States, and a writer of poetry, fiction and non-fiction. He is the author of ten collections of poetry, including *Delights & Shadows* (2004), *Winter Morning Walks: One Hundred Postcards to Jim Harrison* (2000), which won the 2001 Nebraska Book Award for poetry; and *Weather Central* (1994).

Thomas Lux (1946–): Born in Northampton. Massachusetts. His most recent books of poetry include *The Cradle Place* (Houghton Mifflin, 2004), *The Street of Clocks* (2001), and *New and Selected Poems, 1975–1995* (1997), which was a finalist for the 1998 Lenore Marshall Poetry Prize.

Lindsay Macrae (1961–): A Scottish poet, she has had a colorful career spanning television, radio, pop groups, poetry, and cabaret, before writing poetry full time since 1993. *You Canny Shove Yer Granny Off a Bus* (1995) was her first book for children, and *How to Avoid Kissing Your Parents in Public* (2000) won a Scottish Arts Council Children's Book Award.

Jennifer Maier: (1961–) Teaches literature and creative writing at Seattle Pacific University. Maier's poems have appeared in many literary journals—her first poetry collection is called the *School of Weeping*.

Roger McGough (1937–) Born in Liverpool, England. The author of numerous books, he has been publishing his poetry since the 1960s. An award-winning poet, playwright, broadcaster and children's author, McGough is one of Britain's most popular poets.

A. A. Milne (1882–1956): Born in London. In 1906, he became Assistant Editor at *Punch*, the classic British humor magazine. He remained there for the next eight years. A popular playwright, essayist and novelist, he is best remembered for his Winnie-the-Pooh tales for children.

Christian Morgenstern (1871–1914): Born in Munich, Germany. He was a playfully imaginative poet and humorist whose work ranged from the mystical and personally lyrical to nonsense verse.

Ogden Nash (1902–1974): Born in Rye, New York. One of the most widely anthologized comic poets. His first collection of poetry, *Hard Lines* (1931) sold out seven printings in its first year and catapulted Nash into his role as the master of light verse.

Alfred Noyes (1880–1958): Born in Wolverhampton, England. His first collection *The Loom Years* (1903) won him respect from fellow poets W. B. Yeats and George Meredith. Between 1903–1908, Noyes published five volumes of poetry including *The Forest of Wild Thyme* (1905), and *The Flower of Old Japan and Other Poems* (1907). His books were widely reviewed, published, and enjoyed on both sides of the Atlantic.

Frank O'Hara (1926–1966): Born in Baltimore, Maryland. A key member of the New York School of Poets, he worked at the Museum of Modern Art in New York City. His collections include *A City Winter, and Other Poems* (1952), *Meditations in an Emergency* (1956), *Odes* (1960), *Second Avenue* (1960), *Lunch Poems* (1964), and *In Memory of My Feelings* (1967). *The Collected Poems of Frank O'Hara* was published in 1971.

Alicia Suskin Ostriker (1937–) Born in New York. Her books of poems include *The Little Space*: *Poems Selected and New* (1998) and *The Volcano Sequence* (2004). She is also the author of *Stealing the Language,* a germinal critical study of American women's poetry, and of *The Nakedness of the Fathers,* a feminist re-vision of the Old Testament.

Ovid (43 B.C.–A.D. 17): Born in Sulmo in central Italy. A prolific Roman poet whose writing is marked by wit, sophistication, and irreverence. He is best known for his *Amores* and *Metamorphoses*.

Dorothy Parker (1893–1967): Born in New Jersey. A widely anthologized American short story writer, poet, and critic, she was a legendary figure on the New York literary scene. Parker worked for *Vogue, Vanity Fair,* and *The New Yorker*. She later wrote screenplays and helped found the Screen Writers' Guild.

Katha Pollitt (1949–): Highly acclaimed columnist, essay writer and poet, she is well known for her sharp and provocative commentary on popular culture and political issues. She writes a regular column 'Subject to Debate' for *The Nation*, and her poems have been published in *The New Yorker, Harpers, Glamor* and *The New York Times*.

Jack Prelutsky (1940–): Born in Brooklyn, New York. Author of more than thirty poetry collections and anthologies of children's poetry, he devotes much of his time to giving readings at schools and libraries across America. Two of his best known books are *The New Kid on the Block* (1984) and *Something Big Has Been Here* (1990).

Jacques Prévert (1900–1977): Born in Paris. French poet, song and screenplay writer, his collected works are still very popular. *Paroles,* Prévert's first collection of poetry, appeared in 1945. Two further poetry collections, *Soleil de nuit* (1980), and *La cinquième saison* (1984), were published posthumously.

Theodore Roethke (1908–1963): Born in Michigan. A critically acclaimed poet, he was awarded the Pulitzer Prize for Poetry in 1954. Roethke taught at several American Universities, and was mentor to an entire generation of northwest American poets. His collections include *I Am! Says the Lamb* (1961), *Party at the Zoo* (1963), *The Far Field* (1964), *Sequence, Sometimes Metaphysical* (1964), and *Collected Poems* (1966).

Carl Sandburg (1878–): Born in Galesburg, Illinois. One of America's best loved poets, he was a leading light of the Chicago Literary Renaissance. With the appearance of his *Chicago Poems* (1916), *Cornhuskers* (1918), *Smoke and Steel* (1920), and *Slabs of the Sunburnt West* (1922), his reputation was established. He received a second Pulitzer Prize for his *Complete Poems* in 1950. His final volumes of verse were *Harvest Poems, 1910–1960* (1960, and *Honey and Salt* (1963).

May Sarton (1912–1995): Born in Belgium, her family resettled in America. She went on to write popular poetry, novels and her own memoirs. Her poetry collections include *A Durable Fire* (1972), *Halfway to Silence* (1980), *The Silence Now: New and Uncollected Earlier Poems* (1988), *Collected Poems: 1930–1993* (1993), and *Coming Into Eighty* (1994).

James Schevill (1920–): Born in Berkeley, California. Poet, playwright, and Emeritus Professor of English at Brown University. His collections of poetry include *The American Fantasies: Collected Poems 1945–1981* (1983), and *Ambiguous Dancers of Fame: Collected Poems 1945–1985.* (1987).

Percy Bysshe Shelley (1792–1822): Born in Sussex. Quintessential English Romantic poet, and friend of Lord Byron, his rebellious political views and unorthodox lifestyle led him to abandon England for Italy, where Byron was already living.

Lemn Sissay (1967–): Born in Billinge near Wigan, England. Editor, poet, and playwright, he has published a number of collections of poetry including *Rebel Without Applause*. He is also the editor of the highly acclaimed *The Fire People*, a collection of poetry by black British writers (1998).

Stevie Smith (1902–1971): Born in Hull. Yorkshire. A novelist and poet, she worked at a magazine publishing house before retiring to full time writing. Her first collection of verse *A Good Time Was Had By All* (1937), contained her rough sketches or doodles. She did not reach a wide audience until 1962, with the publication of *Selected Poems* and her appearance in the highly regarded Penguin Modern Poets Series. A *Collected Poems* was published in 1975.

Sydney Smith (1771–1845): Born in Woodford, Essex. A leading English wit, also a clergyman and writer, he founded the *Edinburgh Review* in 1802 and became a well known figure in literary society.

Gerald Stern (1925–): Born in Pittsburgh, Pennsylvania. His books of poetry include *Last Blue: Poems* (2000), *This Time: New and Selected Poems* (1998), which won the National Book Award, *Odd Mercy* (1995), *Bread Without Sugar* (1992), winner of the Paterson Poetry Prize; *Leaving Another Kingdom: Selected Poems* (1990), *Two Long Poems* (1990), *Lovesick* (1987), *Paradise Poems* (1984), and *The Red Coal* (1981), which received the Melville Caine Award from the Poetry Society of America. He recently published *American Sonnets* in 2002.

James Stevenson: American poet and illustrator. He has written and/or illustrated more than 100 books for children and lives in Connecticut. His work is regularly featured in the *New York Times*.

Mark Strand (1934–): Born on Prince Edward Island, Canada. Winner of many awards, he has served as Poet Laureate for the United States, and Chancellor of The Academy of American Poets. He is the author of ten books of poems, including *Blizzard of One* (1998), which won the Pulitzer Prize, *Dark Harbor* (1993), *The Continuous Life* (1990), *Selected Poems* (1980), *The Story of Our Lives* (1973), and *Reasons for Moving* (1968).

Ann Taylor (1782–1866): Born in London. English poet, hymn writer, and children's author, she often collaborated with her sister Jane Taylor, perhaps most famously on the rhyme "Twinkle Twinkle Little Star."

William Makepeace Thackeray (1811–1863): Born in Calcutta, India. Mainly known as a novelist and satirist, perhaps most famously for his classic novel *Vanity Fair*, he was also an accomplished poet.

Judith Viorst (1931–): Born in Newark, New Jersey. Author of eight collections of poetry. A graduate of the Washington Psychoanalytic Institute, she has received many awards for her journalism and psychological writings.

Alice Walker (1944–): Born in Eatonton, Georgia. A celebrated author, poet and novelist, her books of poetry include *Her Blue Body Everything We Know: Earthling Poems, 1965–1990 Complete* (1991), *Horses Make the Landscape More Beautiful* (1984), *Goodnight, Willie Lee, I'll See You in the Morning* (1979), *Revolutionary Petunias and Other Poems* (1973), and *Once: Poems* (1968). Her most recent books of poetry are *Absolute Trust in the Goodness of the Earth New Poems* (2003), and *A Poem Traveled Down My Arm: Poems and Drawing* (2003).

Jayne O. Wayne (1938–): American poet living in St. Louis, Missouri. Her book *Strange Heart* (1996) was selected by James Tate for the 1995 Marianne Moore Poetry Prize, and also received the 1996 Society of Midland Authors Poetry Award.

Carolyn Wells (1862–1942): Born in Rahway, New Jersey. A prolific writer, she produced over 170 titles, including children's stories, mystery and detective stories, anthologies, an autobiography, and much humorous and nonsense poetry.

Gail White (1945–): Lives in Breaux Bridge, Louisiana, in the heart of Cajun country. Editor of two poetry anthologies, her own poetry has appeared in a number of magazines, chapbooks, and on two sets of postcards.

Reed Whittemore (1919–): Born in New Haven, Connecticut. He served as the Poet Laureate Consultant in Poetry to the Library of Congress 1984–1985. His collections include *Poems, New and Selected* (1967); *Fifty Poems Fifty* (1970) and *The Past, the Future, the Present: Poems Selected and New* (1990).

Terence Winch: Born in New York. He is the author of *The Drift of Things* (2001), *The Great Indoors* (1995), and *Irish Musicians/American Friends* (1986), which received an American Book Award. His work has appeared in many magazines and anthologies, including the *1997 Best American Poetry*. Winch was awarded an NEA poetry fellowship in 1992.

Sources & Acknowledgements

Kim Addonizio: "What Do Women Want?" from *Tell Me* (BOA Editions, 2000); Jimmy Santiago Baca: 'Listening to Jazz Now' from *Winter Poems Along the Rio Grande* (New Directions, 2004), © 2004 by Jimmy Santiago Baca; Connie Bensley: 'Twelve Things I don't Want to Hear' from *The Back and Front of It* (Bloodaxe Books, 2000), by permission of the publisher; David Berman: 'Snow' from *Actual Air* (Open City Books, 1999), © 1999 by David Berman; Laurel Blossom: 'Fight' from *The Papers Said* (Greenhouse Review Press, 2001), © 2001 by Laurel Blossom, by permission of the publisher; Roy Blount, Jr.: 'Toast to Appetite' from *Soupsongs/Webster's Ark* (Houghton Mifflin, 1987); Palmer Brown: 'The Spangled Pandemonium' from *Spangled Pandemonium: A Colection of Exceptionally Silly Stories & Verses* edited by Fiona Waters (Egmont Books, 1994); Lucille Clifton: 'Praise Song' from *Blessing the Boats: New and Selected Poems 1988–2000* (BOA Editions, 2000), © 2000 by Lucille Clifton; Billy Collins: 'Flames' from *The Apple That Astonished Paris* (University of Arkansas Press, 1988); Wendy Cope: 'English Weather' from *Serious Concerns* (Faber & Faber, 1992); E. E. Cummings: 'maggie and milly and molly and may' from *The Complete Poems 1904–1962*, edited by George J. Firmage (W. W. Norton, 1991), © 1991 by the Trustees for the E. E. Cummings Trust and George J. Firmage; Anna Denise: 'How to Change a Frog Into a Prince; from *The Poets' Grimm: 20th Century Poems from Grimm's Fairy Tales* (Story Line Press, 2003), © 2002 by Anna Denise; Emily Dickinson: 'I'm Nobody! Who are you?' and 'She sights a Bird – she chuckles –' from *The Poems of Emily Dickinson*, edited by Thomas H. Johnson (Cambridge, Massachusetts: The Belknap Press of Harvard University Press), © 1951, 1955, 1979 by the President and Fellows of Harvard College; Gavin Ewart: 'The Young Pobble's Guide to his Toes' from *The Young Pobble's Guide to His Toes* (Hutchinson, 1985) and 'Office Friendships' from *The Gavin Ewart Show: Selected Poems 1939–1985* (Bits Press, 1986), by permission of Margo Ewart; Charlotte Fortune: 'Pls stop sendg msgs 2ths' from *Guardian Online* (30 April 2001); Robert Frost: 'The Objection to Being Stepped On' from *The Poetry of Robert Frost*, edited by Edward Connery Lathem (Jonathan Cape, 1969), © 1962 by Robert Frost, © 1969 by Henry Holt and Company, by permission of Henry Holt and Company, LLC, the Estate of Robert Frost, and The Random House Group Ltd; Harold P. Furth: 'The Perils of Modern Living' from *The New Yorker* (1956); Norman Rowland Gale: 'Bees' from *Collected Poems* (Macmillan, 1914); Faye George: 'Like Anne Shirley's House' first published in *Poetry* (July 1992), reprinted in *Back Roads* (Rock Village Publishing, 2003), © 2003 by Faye George, by permission of the author; Dana Gioia: 'Alley Cat Love Song' from *Interrogations at Noon* (Graywolf Press, 2001), © by Dana Gioia; Beth

Gylys: 'Personal' from *Bodies that Hum* (Silverfish Review Press, 1999); Donald Hall: 'Valentine' from *New Treatury of Children's Poetry: Old Favorites and New Discoveries* compiled by Joanna Cole (Doubleday & Co., 1984); Kaylin Haught: 'God Says Yes To Me' from *The Palm of Your Hand* (Tilbury House Publishers, 1995); Piet Hein: 'Astro-Gymnastics' from *Still More Grooks* (Hodder & Stoughton, 1970), by kind permission of Hugo Piet Hein; Elizabeth Holmes: 'The Fathers' from *Seneca Review, Volume XXXI, No. 1* (Spring 2001), © 2001 by Elizabeth Holmes; David Ignatow: 'The Bagel' from *Rescue the Dead* (University Press of New England, 1968); Issa: 'Haiku' translated by Robert Bly, from *The Sea and the Honeycomb: A book of tiny poems* (Becon Press, 1971); X. J. Kennedy: 'Two Lovers Make Love Despite Their Sunburns' from *Cross Ties: Selected Poems* (University of Georgia Press, 1985) © 1985 by X. J. Kennedy; Galway Kinnell: 'After Making Love We Hear Footsteps' from *Mortal Acts, Mortal Words* (Houghton Mifflin, 1980), © 1980 by Galway Kinnell, by permission of the publisher. All rights reserved; Bill Knott: 'Advice from the Experts' from *Laugh at the End of the World: Collected Comic Poems 1969–1999* (BOA Editions, 2000), © 2000 Bill Knott; Ron Koertge: 'Fault' from *Geography of the Forehead* (University of Arkansas Press, 2000), © 2000 by Ron Koertge; Ted Kooser: 'Selecting a Reader' from *Sure Signs* (University of Pittsburgh Press, 1980), © 1980 by Ted Kooser; 'Dishwater' from *Delights and Shadows* (Copper Canyon Press, 2004); Thomas Lux: "I Love You Sweetheart" from *Split Horizon: Poems* (Houghton Mifflin, 1994), © 1994 Thomas Lux, by permission of Hoghton Mifflin Company All rights reserved; Roger McGough: 'Waving at Trains' from *Waving at Trains* (Jonathan Cape, 1982); Lindsay Macrae: 'Her Latest Flame' from *How to Avoid Kissing Your Parents in Public* (Puffin Books, 2000); Jennifer Maier 'Happiness is Being Danish' from *Swink, Issue 1* (2004), by permission of the author; A. A. Milne: 'Rice Pudding' from *When We Were Very Young* (Methuen Young Books, 1999); Christian Morgenstern: 'Delayed Action' from *Gallows Song*, translated by W. D. Snodgrass and Lore Segal (University of Michigan Press, 1967); Ogden Nash: 'The Chipmunk' 'I Didn't Go To Church Today' 'A Drink With Something In It' and 'Peekabo, I Almost See You' from *Verses from 1929 on* (Little, Brown & Co., 1959), © 1930, 1931, 1934, 1935, 1941 and renewed 1958, 1959, 1962, 1963, and 1969 by Ogden Nash; Alfred Noyes: 'Daddy Fell into the Pond' from *The New Oxford Book of Children's Verse* edited by Neil Philip (Oxford University Press, 1996); Frank O'Hara: 'Poem (Lana Turner has Collapsed!)' from *The Collected Poems of Frank O'Hara* (Alfred A. Knopf, 1970); Alicia Ostriker: 'Summer Haiku' from *Smartish Pace, Issue 9* (2003); Ovid: 'The Amores: Book 1, Poem 3' translated by Peter Green, from *The Erotic Poems* (Penguin Books, 1983); Dorothy Parker: 'One Perfect Rose' and 'The Little Old Lady in Lavender Silk' from *The Collected Dorothy Parker* (Duckworth, 1973), by permission of the publisher; Katha Pollitt: 'Mind Body Problem' from *Antarctic Traveller* (Random House, 1982); Jack Prelutsky: 'Bleezer's Ice Cream' from *The New Kid on the Block* (Greenwillow Books, 1984); Jacques Prévert: 'Freedom Quarter' from *Paroles*, translated by Lawrence Ferlinghetti (City Lights Books, 1967); Theodore Roethke: 'The Sloth' from *The Collected Poems of Theodore Roethke* (Faber & Faber, 1968); Carl Sandburg: 'Happiness' from *Chicago Poems* (Holt, Rinehart & Winston, 1916); May Sarton: 'Eine Kleine Snailmusik' from *The New Yorker* (25 January 1947); James Schevill: 'Green Frog at Roadstead, Wisconsin' from *The American Fantasies: Collected Poems 1945–1981* (Swallow Press, 1983); Lemn Sissay: 'Flowers in the Kitchen' from *Guardian Online* (May 2000), © The Guardian; Stevie Smith: 'Advice to young children' from *The Collected Poems of Stevie Smith* (Penguin Modern Classics, 1985); Gerald Stern: '96 Vandam' from *This Time: New and Selected Poems* (W. W. Norton, 1998); James Stevenson: 'To People I Hear Talking Loudly on Their Cell Phones' from *Corn Chowder* (HarperCollins Children's Books, 2003), © 2003 by James Stevenson; Mark Strand: 'Eating Poetry' from *Reasons for Moving* (Random House, 1992); Judith Viorst: 'True Love' from *It's Hard to be Hip over Thirty and Other Tragedies of Married Life* (Persephone Books, 1999); 'Mother Doesn't Want a Dog' from *If I Were in Charge of the World and Other Worries* (Macmillan, 1981); Alice Walker: 'I'm really very fond' from *Horses Make a Landscape Look More Beautiful* (The Women's Press, 1985); Jane O. Wayne: 'Endangered Species' by permission of the author; 'In Praise of Zigzags' from *A Strange Heart* (Helicon Nine Editions, 1996), by permission of the author; Gail White: 'Ballade of Indignation' from *Light Quarterly, No. 32* (Spring 2001), © 2001 Gail White; Reed Whittemore: 'Spring, Etc' from *The Past, The Future, The Present: Poems Selected and New* (University of Arkansas Press, 1990); Terence Winch: 'Social Security' from *The Paris Review, Volume 42, Number 156* (Fall 2001), © 2001 by Terence Winch.

Every effort has been made to trace or contact copyright holders of the poems published in this book. The editor and publisher apologise for any material included without permission or without the appropriate acknowledgement, and would be glad to rectify any omissions brought to their attention at reprint.

An Hachette UK Company
First published in Great Britain in 2005 by Spruce
a division of Octopus Publishing Group Limited
2–4 Heron Quays, London E14 4JP
www.octopusbooks.co.uk
www.octopusbooksusa.com

Distributed in the U.S. and Canada for Octopus Books USA
c/- Hachette Book Group USA
237 Park Avenue
New York NY 10017

ISBN 13 978-1-84072-667-1
ISBN 10 1-84072-667-9

A CIP catalogue record for this book is available from the
British Library.

Printed and bound in Chine

10 9 8 7 6 5 4 3 2

Jane O. Wayne

The preface to *Poetry to Make you Smile* was written by the poet Jane O. Wayne, whose book, *A Strange Heart*, was selected by James Tate for the 1995 Marianne Moore Poetry Prize, and received the 1996 Society of Midland Authors Poetry Award. Her first book, *Looking Both Ways* received the Devins Award for Poetry. Her poetry has appeared in magazines such as *Poetry*, *Iowa Review*, *The American Scholar*, *The Massachusetts Review*, *Michigan Quarterly Review*, *Poetry Northwest*, *The Wisconsin Review*, and anthologies such as: *Music, Pictures, and Stories*, *Heart to Heart: Poems Inspired by 20th Century Art*, and *The Invisible Ladder*. She has also taught Creative Writing at Webster University and Washington University in St. Louis.

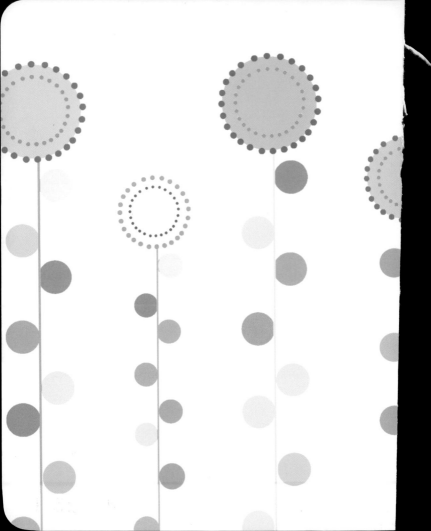